TECH **TITANS**

APPLE

BY JUDY DODGE CUMMINGS

CONTENT CONSULTANT

Anthony Rotolo
Media Scholar, Speaker, and Consultant

Essential Library

An Imprint of Abdo Publishing | abdobooks.com

ABDOBOOKS.COM

Published by Abdo Publishing, a division of ABDO, PO Box 398166, Minneapolis, Minnesota 55439. Copyright © 2019 by Abdo Consulting Group, Inc. International copyrights reserved in all countries. No part of this book may be reproduced in any form without written permission from the publisher. Essential Library™ is a trademark and logo of Abdo Publishing.

Printed in the United States of America, North Mankato, Minnesota.
082018
012019

THIS BOOK CONTAINS
RECYCLED MATERIALS

Cover Photo: Justin Sullivan/Getty Images News/Getty Images
Interior Photos: Yuan Kejia/Imaginechina/AP Images, 4–5; Marcio Jose Sanchez/AP Images, 8, 88–89; Daily Mirror/Mirrorpix/Getty Images, 10–11; Rachel Megawhat/Alamy, 15; Tony Avelar/AP Images for Japan Prize Foundation, 17; Tom Munnecke/Hulton Archive/Getty Images, 21; Xerox/Getty Images News/Getty Images, 22–23; Ted Thai/The LIFE Picture Collection/Getty Images, 25; Sal Veder/AP Images, 27; Paul Sakuma/AP Images, 33, 42, 53, 55, 67, 68–69, 77; PlusONE/Shutterstock Images, 35 (left); Shutterstock Images, 35 (right); Eric Sander/Liaison/Hulton Archive/Getty Images, 36–37; Julia Malakie/AP Images, 44–45, 48; David Paul Morris/Getty Images News/Getty Images, 56–57; Anton Ivanov/Shutterstock Images, 59; Red Line Editorial, 62, 92; Julie Jacobson/AP Images, 65; Denys Prykhodov/Shutterstock Images, 74; Carolyn Kaster/AP Images, 78–79; Yuan Shuiling/Imaginechina/AP Images, 83; J. Scott Applewhite/AP Images, 86; Justin Sullivan/Getty Images News/Getty Images, 97

Editor: Arnold Ringstad
Series Designer: Laura Polzin

Library of Congress Control Number: 2018948252

Publisher's Cataloging-in-Publication Data

Names: Dodge Cummings, Judy, author.
Title: Apple / by Judy Dodge Cummings.
Description: Minneapolis, Minnesota : Abdo Publishing, 2019 | Series: Tech titans | Includes online resources and index.
Identifiers: ISBN 9781532116865 (lib. bdg.) | ISBN 9781532159701 (ebook)
Subjects: LCSH: Apple Computer, Inc.--Juvenile literature. | iPhone (Smartphone)--Juvenile literature. | Music retailers--Juvenile literature. | Technology--Juvenile literature.
Classification: DDC 338.470040--dc23

CONTENTS

CHAPTER **ONE**

FIRST IN LINE

On November 2, 2017, an odd scene played out in front of Apple Stores around the world. In Chicago, Illinois, a customer walked up to the Apple Store on North Michigan Avenue at 11:00 a.m. However, he did not enter the building. Instead, the customer stood outside, waiting. Over the next 12 hours, more than 200 people joined him. In New York City, campsites popped up on the sidewalks in front of Apple Stores. As darkness fell, people stretched out on air mattresses or lawn chairs or crawled into small tents. Similar lines stretched in front of Apple Stores from London, England, to Sydney, Australia, to Hong Kong and beyond.

Apple employees are used to this phenomenon. The folks waiting outside the stores are their most loyal customers. These die-hard followers were waiting for the stores to open at 8:00 a.m. on November 3. That was when a radically redesigned smartphone, the

For years, Apple fans have lined up on release day to get the latest version of the iPhone.

iPhone X, would be available for the first time. This device, with a starting price of $999, was guaranteed to fly off the shelves. For years, Apple devotees have endured lack of sleep, no bathrooms, and the wind, rain, and snow to get their hands on the company's latest devices. Apple's mix of advanced technology with sleek design has won it millions of fans over the past four decades.

When the Chicago Apple Store finally opened its doors on November 3, Kapish Sharma was the sixth person to enter the store. He had driven up from Indiana and stood in line for 15 hours. "Our wait was worth it," Sharma said as he walked out of the store with an iPhone X in his hand.[1]

iPHONE X

From 2007 until 2017, every iPhone shared the same basic design: a large screen with space above it for a speaker and space below it for a single physical button. The iPhone X was the first significant departure from this style. The phone's screen goes from edge to edge with almost no border. There is no longer a physical button below the screen. At the top of the screen is a small cutout notch containing a speaker, cameras, and sensors. Previous iPhones were unlocked with the user's fingerprint on the single button below the screen. The iPhone X instead unlocks when its cameras recognize the user's face.

THE RACE TO $1 TRILLION

Apple has many loyal fans, and its products have found mainstream success around the globe. On January 17,

2018, Apple was valued at $911.906 billion, more than any company in world history.[2] Other tech giants are racing to catch Apple, each one vying to be the first publicly traded corporation worth $1 trillion.

One reason for Apple's success is what industry experts call the Apple ecosystem. Apple sells hardware devices, including smartphones, laptops, and tablets. It also designs the operating systems that run on these devices, meaning that the hardware and software are created to work well together. The more Apple products a person has, the more benefits he or she gets. A person with both an iPhone and a MacBook laptop can use text messaging on both devices. People who buy music on the iTunes Store can listen to it across all their Apple devices. User data, including photos, emails, and lists of contacts, is easily shared across Apple smartphones, tablets, and computers. The interconnectedness of this ecosystem encourages users to stick with Apple products. Having one Apple product can make it more enticing to buy another. The result is highly profitable for Apple.

Apple is a resilient company that has ridden a roller coaster of dizzying success and near catastrophic failure for 40 years. The company was founded by two young

Apple touts its latest software and hardware at major presentations put on for the press, software developers, and the public.

men in 1976. Steve Wozniak was an engineering prodigy and Steve Jobs a marketing mastermind. After successfully transforming the world of personal computers with the Apple II and the Macintosh, Wozniak left the company to pursue other dreams. Jobs was forced out of the company because of his management style. But without Jobs's vision, the company struggled. In 1997, Jobs returned to Apple and took the company from near bankruptcy to record profitability with the iPod and iPhone.

After Jobs died in 2011, Tim Cook became Apple's chief executive officer. He had a rocky start. The company faced controversies related to user privacy and taxes in Cook's first few years at the helm. But Cook successfully steered Apple through these storms. Today Apple stands as a titan of technology because of its trademark combination of revolutionary technical innovations with award-winning product designs. Apple is poised to carry this pioneering spirit into the future.

BATTERY SLOWDOWN

In the fall of 2017, people noticed their older iPhones ran noticeably faster after their batteries were replaced. This suggested that the phones were intentionally running slower with the old batteries. Users accused Apple of intentionally slowing down old iPhone models when new iPhones were released, forcing users to buy a new phone. When a software company ran tests and confirmed the slowdowns, Apple was forced to publicly address the issue. The company explained that batteries lose capacity over time. When a battery deteriorates to a certain level, it may cause a phone to shut down unexpectedly. To prevent this, the software slows down the phone's processor so that it doesn't demand as much power. This stops the phone from shutting down, but it also slows down the phone. "We know that some of you feel Apple has let you down," the company said in a press release. "We apologize."[3] Apple offered a steep discount on replacement batteries for the older phones. However, many users felt deceived.

CHAPTER TWO

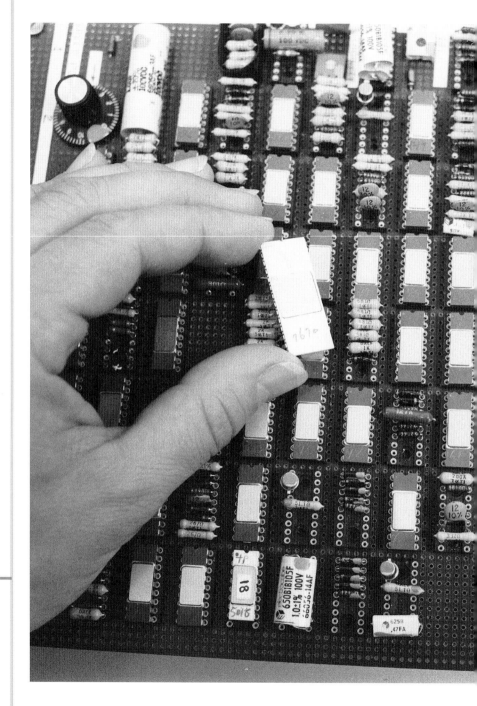

APPLE'S ROOTS

I n the 1950s, the apricot and peach orchards along the southern portion of the San Francisco Bay gave way to manufacturers of silicon chips. These components were the building blocks of the computer industry. Companies that relied on silicon moved their headquarters to the region, and a journalist dubbed the area Silicon Valley. Engineers, chemists, and computer programmers came to the valley for jobs. For kids who loved math and science, it was the perfect place to grow up. Two of these kids were Stephen Wozniak and Steve Jobs.

THE TWO STEVES MEET

Stephen "Woz" Wozniak was born in 1950 in the heart of Silicon Valley. His father, an engineer, taught Wozniak about electronics before the boy could read. When Wozniak was ten, his goal was to own his own computer. In his senior year in

Silicon Valley, with its new industrial growth centered on the silicon chip, became the birthplace for many of today's best-known technology companies, including Apple.

high school, Wozniak worked at an electronics company and learned computer programming. In his spare time, he studied manuals for small computers, challenging himself to redesign them with fewer parts.

Steve Jobs was born in 1955 and moved to Los Altos, California, with his adoptive family when he was in seventh grade. His father, a craftsman, taught Jobs to pay as much attention to the underside of a cabinet, even though it would never be seen, as to its surface.

Jobs joined the Explorer's Club, a group of teens who met on the campus of technology company Hewlett-Packard (HP) to work on electronics projects. When he was 12, Jobs wanted to build a device called a frequency counter but he did not have a key part. Assuming Bill Hewlett, the founder and chief executive officer (CEO) of HP, would have the necessary part, Jobs called the boss at home. Hewlett not only gave Jobs the part but also hired the boy for a summer job.

The two Steves met in 1971. Wozniak was a 20-year-old sophomore at De Anza College, and Jobs was 17 and still in high school. Wozniak and Jobs were unaware that they shared a common friend—16-year-old Bill Fernandez. One day when Fernandez and Jobs were hanging out, they ran into Wozniak washing his car. "They might be interested in meeting each other and doing electronics stuff," Fernandez figured.[1]

THE PARTNERSHIP

Financial pressures forced Wozniak to drop out of college at the end of his junior year, and his friendship with Jobs waned. Wozniak was hired by HP to work on scientific calculators. Jobs graduated from high school in 1972 and attended one semester of college. He dropped out to travel, but he wound up back in his parents' house because he was broke. In 1973, Jobs got a low-level job at the early video game company Atari.

AN ILLEGAL PROJECT

The first joint technology project between Wozniak and Jobs was illegal. In the 1970s, the only telephones were landlines, and calling long distance was expensive. In 1971, Wozniak read a magazine story about hackers who had built a device called a blue box that avoided long-distance charges by mimicking the tones used by the phone company for dialed numbers. Wozniak invented an improved digital blue box.

Jobs saw the blue boxes as a chance to make money. He and Wozniak manufactured dozens and sold them in Wozniak's dorm. Each box cost $40 to make and sold for $150. Wozniak and Jobs split the profits. This experience taught the men how to work together and successfully market a product. In 1996, Jobs said, "I don't think there would ever have been an Apple computer had there not been blue boxes."[2]

One day, Jobs called Wozniak with a proposition. His boss wanted him to design and code a video game, and Jobs needed help. There was one hitch. They had to design the game in only four days. The men worked around the clock and met the deadline. Their friendship was rekindled.

THE SEED SPROUTS

One night in March 1975, Wozniak attended his first meeting of the Homebrew Club, a group of people interested in technology that met every Wednesday night. One club member had just purchased the Altair 8800. Built from a kit, this simple home computer had rows of toggle switches and blinking red lights. Wozniak took a copy of its schematics home.

The computer thrilled Wozniak, but the toggle switches and flashing lights seemed so old fashioned. Why not enter commands and data on a keyboard? Why not program the computer to project results on a TV monitor? "That night," Wozniak recalled, "this whole vision of a . . . personal computer just popped into my head."[3]

THE PROTOTYPE

On June 29, 1975, Wozniak built a computer. He turned it on and typed random letters on the attached keyboard. To his joy, the letters appeared on the television screen he

The Altair 8800 inspired Wozniak to improve upon it and make a computer that was easier to use.

had hooked into the circuit board. This was the first time in history that someone had typed on a keyboard and had the letters show up instantly on a screen.

Wozniak often brought his prototype to Homebrew Club meetings, and Jobs sometimes tagged along. Hoping other members would build their own machines, Wozniak freely handed out the computer's schematics. That fall, Jobs told Wozniak that some club members wanted a computer but did not have the time or knowledge to build one themselves. "Why don't we build and then sell the printed circuit boards to them?" Jobs asked. "We could make them for $20 each and sell them for $40."[4]

But it would cost $1,000 to hire a company to print the circuit boards. To get the $1,000, Jobs sold his van and Wozniak sold his scientific calculator. Soon they had sold a few dozen circuit boards to some Homebrew members for a small profit. Jobs and Wozniak brought Ron Wayne into their business. He was a skilled technical and legal writer who worked at Atari. Jobs and Wozniak gave Wayne 10 percent of the company.[5] One day, as Wozniak and Jobs were returning from a visit to Oregon, the men brainstormed names for their business. Jobs suggested the name Apple Computer. It was simple, understandable, and relatable, like the computers they wanted to build. On April 1, 1976, the men registered Apple Computer Company as a California business partnership.

Wozniak's final prototype, called Apple I, did not resemble today's computers, but it was radical for its time. The circuit board contained 60 silicon chips and a power supply. The board could be connected to a keyboard and monitor. Wozniak wrote a version of BASIC, a simple programming language, to run on Apple I's microprocessor.

The day Wozniak and Jobs showed off the prototype at the Homebrew Club, one man showed interest. Paul

Some surviving Apple I computers can be seen in museums.

Terrell owned a computer store called the Byte Shop, and he told the men he would like to talk business with them someday. To Jobs, "someday" meant immediately. The next morning he borrowed a car and drove to the Byte Shop. That afternoon, Wozniak was at work when his phone rang. "Guess what?" Jobs asked. "I've got a $50,000 order."[6] Terrell had ordered 100 Apple I computers at $500 each.

Neither Wozniak nor Jobs had the money to build 100 computers. They begged and borrowed and bought on credit to get the necessary parts. Then Jobs hired friends to plug memory chips into sockets on the circuit boards. The Jobs family garage became Apple's factory. Wozniak tested each circuit board by plugging it into a television and keyboard. Then Jobs drove the finished boards to the Byte Shop, where Terrell paid him in cash.

By early 1976, Apple was making a small profit as Wozniak and Jobs drove around California selling their machines at computer stores. Jobs was 21 and still lived with his parents, and Wozniak was 25 and still worked at HP. The men enjoyed the extra money, but Wayne was not having fun. Used to big companies and a steady salary, Wayne sold his share of Apple to his partners for $800.[7]

Wozniak knew he could build a better computer, but that would require a lot of money. At this point, the complementary parts of the Wozniak and Jobs partnership became apparent. While Wozniak engineered a better machine, Jobs found funding.

APPLE II

Jobs could be persuasive and charismatic, but sometimes his scruffy, long-haired look made professional businessmen leery of making deals with Apple. Jobs's funding pitch was turned down by Atari, Commodore, and

Sequoia Capital. Eventually someone introduced him to A. C. "Mike" Markkula, a millionaire and former executive at computer chip maker Intel.

Markkula recognized Apple's potential and invested $92,000 of his own money. In return, he received one-third of Apple's stock and was named chairman of the board. Markkula also insisted that Wozniak quit his job at HP and work for Apple full time. Then Markkula hired Michael "Scotty" Scott, a 32-year-old manufacturing manager, as Apple's first CEO.

Apple moved into a real office in Cupertino, California, where Wozniak built a prototype of the Apple II. The team decided to announce it at a computer fair in San Francisco on April 16, 1977. Apple II had a faster processor and more memory than Apple I, and it came with color graphics, an audio amplifier, a speaker, and eight expansion

INTRODUCING THE APPLE II

When the 1977 computer fair opened, 12,000 people flooded into San Francisco's civic center to see the new personal computer.[8] The Apple booth had a counter draped in black velvet and a pane of backlit Plexiglas that displayed the new Apple logo. On the counter sat Apple II, the most complete personal computer available. Whereas other computers looked like pieces of mechanical equipment, Apple II was housed in a sleek, beige case and resembled a small appliance. The company received 300 orders during the fair.[9]

slots so the machine could be expanded to add memory or new hardware.

The company was soon selling modest numbers of Apple II computers each month, but in 1979 everything changed. The software developer VisiCorp released VisiCalc, the first spreadsheet computer program, for the Apple II. The software became invaluable for businesses, and sales of Apple II computers skyrocketed from $7.8 million in 1978 to $117.9 million in 1980.[10]

On December 12, 1980, Apple stock was sold on the New York Stock Exchange for the first time, and it was one of the most successful initial stock sales in history. In 1977, Apple was worth $5,309. By the end of 1980, the company was valued at $1.79 billion.[11]

STEPHEN WOZNIAK

When Stephen Wozniak was a kid, he was a science fair champion. Wozniak built a flashlight, an electronic model of the periodic table, and a calculator called the Adder/Subtractor. These projects taught Wozniak patience. "Throughout my career at Apple and other places," he wrote, "you always find . . . geeks who try to reach levels without doing the in-between ones first, and it won't work. . . . One step at a time."[12]

After the success of Apple II, Wozniak continued to improve the machine, but Jobs wanted Wozniak to work on a new computer, the Macintosh. Before Wozniak could get involved in the Macintosh project, he crashed his new single-engine plane on February 7, 1981. Wozniak barely survived, and he suffered from partial amnesia for months. When he recovered, he decided to move on with his life. He enrolled in college to finish his degree.

Wozniak remained a part-time spokesman for Apple while pursuing other interests. He started a company that designed a remote control device and spent ten years teaching computer classes to elementary students. In 2009, Wozniak played against the stereotype of a computer nerd by performing on the television show *Dancing with the Stars*. He continued to work for a variety of technology companies.

Wozniak led the engineering efforts on Apple's early products.

CHAPTER THREE

FAILURE AND SUCCESS

In 1979, Jobs got to tour a place that outsiders rarely saw. This visit transformed the computer industry. Xerox Corporation, best known for its copying machines, dominated innovation in Silicon Valley in the 1970s, and it wanted to invest in Apple Computer. Jobs offered Xerox 100,000 shares for $1 million, if he was given a tour of the company's Palo Alto Research Center (PARC), the part of Xerox where all the company's research and development was done.[1] Xerox agreed.

During the tour, Jobs saw the Alto, the personal computer Xerox was developing. At a time when moving a cursor required the user to type a command on a keyboard, Jobs was amazed by a tool Xerox had invented. They called it a mouse. Moving the mouse would move a cursor around the display. A click on an icon

Xerox PARC was the birthplace of many features that computer users take for granted today.

would open and close programs. In addition, Xerox had developed a program that allowed Alto users to send messages to other people inside Xerox. Jobs realized that such innovations would soon change the entire computer industry.

DESIGN FAILURES

International Business Machines (IBM) had been making adding machines, calculators, and mainframe computers for governments and corporations since 1911. When the market for personal computers became profitable in the late 1970s, IBM began developing its own model. Apple wanted to introduce a personal computer to meet the needs of corporations before IBM got there first. By the fall of 1979, Apple was simultaneously developing three possible successors to Apple II—the Apple III, the Lisa, and the Macintosh.

The Apple III was released on May 19, 1980. Wozniak had not designed this computer, and his absence showed. The Apple III had more memory than the Apple II, but Jobs's desire for an elegant design trumped function. Jobs wanted the machine small and silent. Engineers struggled to build the computer in a way that the inside would not overheat without a noisy fan. In the end, the business

Jobs showed off the Lisa for the press in 1983.

community did not want Apple III. It was expensive, starting at more than $4,000, and it was unreliable.[2] The motherboard overheated and warped, causing chips to pop out of their sockets. Apple advised customers to pick up the computer and drop it a few inches to reset the chips.

Lisa would not be the breakthrough Apple needed, either. The machine was originally designed for corporations that needed to process massive amounts of data, but Jobs had a different vision when he took over the project. He made the computer better for personal use, incorporating overlapping windows and a mouse, innovations he had taken from Xerox PARC. However, these changes slowed down development and raised the cost.

CEO Scott realized Lisa was far behind deadline and would be too expensive to dominate the business market. In the fall of 1980, he removed Jobs from the project. As Apple's stock value declined, the pressure on Scott grew. His leadership veered from bullying people one minute to babying them the next. In March 1981, Scott laid off 40 people at a company-wide meeting, including half of Apple's engineers.[3] The board lost confidence in Scott, and he resigned on July 10, 1981.

DO OR DIE

Following Scott's departure, Markkula became the interim CEO, and Jobs took over as the chairman. This shake-up at the top occurred only weeks before IBM blindsided Apple.

In August 1981, IBM released the IBM Personal Computer (PC). Rather than use its own patented hardware, IBM built the PC from readily available parts.

This meant other computer manufacturers could build copycat machines, and they did. Retailing at $1,565, the PC was much cheaper than the Apple III.[4] When IBM introduced its own spreadsheet program to rival Apple's VisiCalc, businesses turned to the IBM PC for their computing needs. Apple had lost its chance to dominate the personal computer market.

Apple's leadership knew that changes would need to be made. To fill the position of permanent CEO, Jobs wanted John Sculley, the head of Pepsi. Sculley initially declined the offer, but Jobs refused to take no for an

Sculley, *center*, joined Jobs and Wozniak in 1983.

answer. "Do you want to sell sugar water for the rest of your life?" he asked. "Or do you want to come with me and change the world?"[5] Sculley took the job.

After Jobs was removed from the Lisa team, he focused on a project led by Jef Raskin, a former college professor. Raskin was designing a low-cost personal computer called the Macintosh. Still eager to build a computer with features like Xerox's Alto, Jobs said Raskin's design was "all wrong."[6] He undercut Raskin at every turn and eventually took control of the project. Raskin quit.

Under Jobs's leadership, the Macintosh project was kept separate from the rest of Apple. Jobs kept the number of team members under 100 so he could remember everyone's names. The average age of the staff was under 30, and the uniform was jeans and T-shirts. The Macintosh team worked in its own building. A pirate flag flew from the roof, and the lobby had video games, a stereo, a grand piano, and a BMW motorcycle. Jobs believed these items inspired creativity and craftsmanship.

For two years, the Mac team worked constantly. It was a do-or-die moment for Apple. The popularity of IBM PCs was growing, and the development of the Macintosh was gobbling up Apple's cash reserves. Jobs had staked his reputation and Apple's value on this product. "If we don't do this," Jobs said, "nobody can stop IBM."[7] Finally, the Macintosh prototype was ready, and the time came to announce the news to the world.

1984

On January 22, 1984, the LA Raiders were trouncing the Washington Redskins in Super Bowl XVIII. During a commercial break in the third quarter, audiences across the United States watched a 60-second story unfold on their televisions.

Bald, human drones in striped uniforms marched inside tubes that twisted through a cavernous building. The scene shifted. A woman clad in red shorts and a white tank top sprinted into the scene, her shorts the only spot of color in the drab world. The runner carried a sledgehammer.

STEALING FROM THE NEIGHBORS

In 1983, Bill Gates announced that Microsoft was developing an operating system for IBM PCs that would help PCs compete with the Macintosh. Jobs was livid. "Get Gates down here immediately," he ordered. When Gates arrived, Jobs accused him, "You're ripping us off!" Gates replied, "Well, Steve . . . I think it's more like we both had this rich neighbor named Xerox and I broke into the house to steal the TV set and found out that you had already stolen it."[8]

The drones entered an auditorium. On a huge screen at the front of the room was the face of a man whose voice was echoing throughout the building. The scene was reminiscent of the George Orwell novel *1984*. The drones sat on benches, eyes glazed as they stared at their leader. Suddenly, the hammer-wielding woman charged into the room. She raced up the center aisle and hurled the hammer into the giant screen. The room exploded into light. At this point in the commercial, words scrolled across the screen, along with matching narration: "On January 24th, Apple Computer will introduce Macintosh. And you'll see why 1984 won't be like *1984*."[9]

With that, the commercial ended. This advertisement was Apple's warning that it was about to start a revolution. Users of ordinary PCs were shown as drones. The Macintosh was presented as an incredible new direction for computers.

Two days later, Jobs officially launched the Macintosh at a shareholders' meeting on the campus of De Anza College in Cupertino. In his speech, Jobs told the story of IBM's efforts to dominate the personal computer market. He painted the competition between IBM and Apple as a battle for the soul of the industry. Near the end of the speech, Jobs removed the black bag that had covered a Macintosh on a table in the center of the stage. As the machine came to life, words appeared on the monitor as if being written by an invisible hand: "MACINTOSH. Insanely Great."

Jobs explained the Mac's different features and then said, "I'd like to let Macintosh speak for itself." In a robotic voice, the computer said, "Hello. I am Macintosh. It sure is great to get out of that bag."[11] The crowd went wild.

The Macintosh was groundbreaking. It cost $2,500, a reasonable price in the early 1980s.[12] The Mac was the first mainstream computer with a graphical user interface, meaning the user moved a mouse to manipulate and select things, rather than typing in commands on an all-text screen. A paintbrush icon brought up a drawing program. For a document, select a file folder. No other personal computer, including IBM's, could do all of these things.

Software and marketing helped sell the Macintosh. Apple pumped $20 million into television ads in 1984 and recruited outside companies to write Mac software. One of these companies was Microsoft, run by Bill Gates. Gates praised Apple's new computer and said it had created a new standard in personal computers. But this partnership between Apple and Microsoft would soon sour.

JOBS'S TROUBLES

After the successful launch of Macintosh, Jobs became a kind of celebrity, but inside the company people resented how he treated them. The Lisa and Macintosh teams were combined, and Sculley put Jobs in charge. Jobs explained to both teams why he was giving all the top positions to the Mac team. "You guys failed," he told the people who had worked on Lisa. "You're a B team. B players."[13]

Jobs's arrogance rubbed people the wrong way. He alienated software developers like Gates by making it seem like he was doing them a favor by letting them develop programs for the Macintosh. Gates recalled that when he visited Apple's headquarters, Jobs told the

Microsoft team, "This thing [Macintosh] is so cool, I don't even know why I'm going to let you guys have anything to do with this. . . . I heard what a bunch of idiots you guys are."[14] At the time, Microsoft was still a small company, but it would not be for long.

Soon Jobs would have little to brag about. In the second half of 1984, Macintosh sales dropped significantly. The Mac was too slow. The graphical user interface made the computer fun to use, but it required

Apple produced its Macintosh computers at a factory in California.

a lot of memory. In order to keep the cost and size of the Mac down, engineers had not designed it with much memory. Tensions between Sculley and Jobs grew.

Then Jobs made a series of poor decisions. He took the unsold Lisas, modified them to run Mac software, and labeled the machines Macintosh XL. No one believed this was a brand-new model. Jobs also backed a 1985 Super Bowl commercial that characterized IBM PC users as lemmings, stupid birds mindlessly marching off a cliff to their deaths. The commercial insulted business leaders, the very people Apple was trying to attract.

The managers of other departments put pressure on John Sculley to do something about Jobs. Finally, one evening in March 1985, the CEO acted. Sculley went to Jobs's office. He began, "There is no one who admires your brilliance and vision more than I do, but . . . I have lost confidence in your ability to run the Macintosh division."[15] He told Jobs he intended to recommend to the board of directors that Jobs be removed from the Mac team. Jobs was stunned. First, he lashed out, and then he began to cry. But Sculley did not change his mind.

At a board meeting on April 11, 1985, the directors sided with Sculley. Jobs asked that his transition away

MACINTOSH (1984)
SCREEN SIZE: 9 INCHES (23 CM)
SCREEN RESOLUTION: 512 X 342
PROCESSOR SPEED: 8 MHZ
MEMORY: 1 MB
BUILT-IN STORAGE: NONE

iMAC (2018)
SCREEN SIZE: 21.5 INCHES (55 CM)
SCREEN RESOLUTION: 4096 X 2304
PROCESSOR SPEED: 3.4 GHZ
MEMORY: 8 GB
BUILT-IN STORAGE: 1 TB

from the Macintosh division be gradual, and Sculley agreed. But over the next few weeks, Jobs badgered the CEO constantly for more time to prove himself. Sculley refused, so Jobs decided to take drastic action. He made plans to overthrow Apple's CEO.

CHAPTER **FOUR**

A BRUISED APPLE

Over Memorial Day weekend in 1985, Sculley was supposed to fly to China for a meeting. However, someone informed him that Jobs intended to "launch a coup" while Sculley was out of the country.[1] Sculley canceled the trip, and on Friday, May 24, he confronted Jobs at an executive staff meeting. Sculley told the executive committee they had to choose between him or Jobs. One by one, the board members sided with Sculley. Jobs returned to his office and cried.

On May 31, Jobs sat in Apple's auditorium as Sculley announced a reorganization. Jean-Louis Gassée, the director of European operations, replaced Jobs as head of the Macintosh division. Jobs was made chairman of the board. He had a title but no power.

Jobs endured this situation for a few months, but on September 17 he submitted a letter of resignation. "The company's recent

With Jobs gone, Sculley took responsibility for shaping Apple's strategy starting in the mid-1980s.

reorganization left me with no work to do. . . . I am but 30 and want still to contribute and achieve."[2] Then Jobs walked away from the company he had founded.

LEADERSHIP TROUBLES

After Jobs's resignation, Apple's stock rose. Now Apple would be managed more traditionally. Sculley had a different vision of the kind of company Apple should be. Jobs had dreamed of Apple becoming a consumer products company. In 1987, Sculley wrote, "This was a lunatic plan. . . . High tech could not be designed and sold as a consumer product."[3]

For a while, Sculley managed Apple effectively. He reorganized the company for efficiency. Previously, Apple had been structured by product. Each division had its own independent marketing and design team. Marketers and engineers from different divisions vied for funding for their projects. Sculley changed this system by combining divisions based on function. All product development took place in one division. All marketing happened within another. Engineers were ordered to collaborate with marketers. All division heads reported directly to Sculley.

Apple remained financially stable in the mid-1980s. The Macintosh dominated the desktop publishing market and made Apple a lot of money. But when Microsoft developed a new operating system that eventually became successful, Apple's finances slipped.

JOBS ON MICROSOFT

Jobs frequently had harsh words to say about Microsoft. In a 1996 documentary, Jobs said, "The only problem with Microsoft is they just have . . . absolutely no taste."[4] In 2007, moments before taking the stage with Gates for a joint interview, Jobs told a journalist that Apple had designed its music software, iTunes, to run on PCs with Windows because it was "like giving a glass of ice water to somebody in hell."[5]

Microsoft had released the first version of its operating system, Windows 1.0, in the fall of 1984. This system ran on IBM PCs and featured a graphical interface with windows and icons. However, Windows 1.0 was clumsy and unpopular, and Apple did not view it as a threat. But while Gates led Microsoft to improve Windows, Sculley did little to update the Mac's operating system. In 1990, Microsoft released Windows 3.0, a much better version. Slowly, PCs running Windows computers consumed more of the personal computer market.

Under Sculley, Apple lost its focus. Nine different computer models were available by 1989. Developing this many models cost Apple millions of dollars in research. However, the computers were expensive to purchase and did not sell well.

Sculley was convinced Apple had a hit with a device called the Newton. This handheld device was billed as a personal assistant. Its star application was Notes, in which users could write on the screen with a stylus and have their writing converted to text. But the device flopped. The failure of the Newton sealed Sculley's fate. Apple's board of directors decided the time had come for him to go. Under pressure, Sculley resigned in 1993.

Sculley was replaced with Michael Spindler, the head of Apple's European operations. Spindler tried to fend off Microsoft's takeover of the computer market by licensing the Macintosh operating system to other manufacturers.

THE NEWTON

Sculley announced the Newton in 1992 and toured the world promoting it. However, he had announced the device before it was ready. Scheduled for release in April 1992, the Newton saw its release date pushed back to August 1993. Engineers pushed through brutal 18-hour days trying to get it ready.

Despite these sacrifices, the Newton had serious flaws when it finally reached stores. The handwriting program Sculley had boasted about inaccurately translated people's notes, and the Newton cost $699, far more than people were willing to spend for an unreliable device. Four months after the release, only $50,000 worth of Newtons had been sold.[6]

However, when these companies produced poor-quality computers, people assumed they were Apple products and the company's reputation suffered.

The tipping point for Apple's bottom line was Microsoft's release of Windows 95 on August 24, 1995. It was faster and more reliable than the Macintosh operating system. It became a massive success. Microsoft's operating system ran on any PC, while Apple's Macintosh operating system ran only on Apple computers. This meant the potential market for Windows was much larger. In the late 1980s, Apple had controlled 16 percent of the personal computer market. By 1996, it controlled only 4 percent. Spindler tried to sell Apple to IBM and HP, but neither company wanted it. That year the board fired Spindler and hired one of its own members, Gil Amelio, to replace him.

Amelio was a research engineer and had been the CEO of National Semiconductor. He had his work cut out for him. Apple was on the brink of bankruptcy. In fiscal year 1995, Apple made $11.1 billion in sales. By 1996, this had shrunk to $9 billion.[7] Amelio brought in a new chief financial officer, Fred Anderson. Working together, the

Amelio took drastic measures to try to reverse Apple's downward spiral in the mid-1990s.

new leaders tried to stop the hemorrhage of money. They laid off 2,800 employees and cut operating costs.[8]

However, new computer buyers were still choosing PCs over Macs. Amelio knew Apple desperately needed a new operating system, something that could rival Windows. However, the company did not have the time to do this before it ran out of money. In the first quarter of 1996, Apple posted a loss, and creditors were demanding repayment of loans. If immediate action was not taken, Apple could go out of business.

A NEW OPERATING SYSTEM

Amelio knew of one company that could supply a new operating system for Apple: NeXT. The company had been founded by Jobs in 1988 after he left Apple. Jobs's initial goal was to build workstations for universities, powerful machines with the friendly features of a personal computer. However, NeXT's computers cost more than educational institutions wanted to pay, and there was not much available software. Jobs instead focused on licensing the NeXTSTEP operating system to run on other computers. Apple needed NeXTSTEP, but Amelio did not want to call Jobs and beg for help.

Unknown to Amelio, a mid-level marketer at NeXT had already contacted a friend at Apple to see if she might be interested in NeXT's software. Negotiations took place, and by December 2, 1996, Jobs was in a conference room at Apple's headquarters making a pitch to Amelio.

A week later, Apple's board of directors approved the purchase of NeXT for more than $400 million. Amelio would not give Jobs a spot on Apple's board, but when Jobs asked to be named adviser to the chairman, Amelio agreed. Eleven years after Jobs had been pushed out of Apple, he was back. But Apple was a very different company than when Jobs had left. Even with its founder back, Apple could still fail.

CHAPTER FIVE

REGENERATION

I n his first few months back with Apple, Jobs was unhappy with how Amelio was running the company. Jobs later told his biographer, "I thought he [Amelio] was a bozo."[1] Jobs was not the only one. Chief financial officer Anderson told chairman of the board Edgar Woolard Jr. that if the company kept Amelio in charge, Apple had a slim chance of avoiding bankruptcy. On July 4, 1997, Woolard fired Amelio.

Woolard immediately offered the position of CEO to Jobs. Jobs turned it down. However, he agreed to advise Apple and help recruit a new CEO. Woolard informed Apple's executives that Anderson would serve as interim CEO, but that Jobs "would be an advisor leading the team."[2] Jobs stood up to address the managers. He was casually dressed in shorts, sneakers, and his signature black turtleneck. "Okay, tell me what's wrong with this place," he asked the

Jobs's return to Apple delighted many longtime fans of the company, but he had significant work to do in turning Apple around.

FOUR PRODUCTS

One day, as the executive team was hashing out ideas for products, Jobs shouted, "Enough!" He walked to a whiteboard and drew a grid with four squares. Jobs labeled the columns "consumer" and "pro" and the rows "desktop" and "portable." This was Apple's mission, Jobs said. The company would make only four great products, one to fit each square. The executive team sat in stunned silence at the simplicity of his vision. This business model ultimately saved Apple. But first a lot of work had to be done, starting with a rebranding of the company.

group before immediately answering his own question. "It's the products. . . . The products suck!"[3] Before Apple could create better products, it first had to get on solid financial footing.

A NEW PLAN AND A NEW PARTNERSHIP

Jobs scrutinized every aspect of Apple, from product design to advertising to employee turnover, and then made sweeping changes. He told Chairman Woolard he did not have time to deal with the board. Then Jobs demanded every board member except Woolard resign. He recruited new board members, naming himself as one, too. Word spread that Jobs was deeply engaged in the day-to-day work of the company, and Apple stock jumped from $13 a share to $20 in July 1997.[4]

One month later, thousands of Apple fans converged on Boston, Massachusetts, for the annual Macworld trade show. Jobs came onstage to give the keynote speech to a crowd chanting "Steve! Steve! Steve!" For 30 minutes he spoke about what he believed had gone wrong with Apple. He explained that Apple had to refocus its brand. The people who bought Apple products were different, he said. They were "creative spirits . . . out to change the world." Apple's mission was to make "tools for those kinds of people."[5] Some members of the audience wept. Their visionary leader was back.

But those tears turned to jeers near the end of Jobs's speech when he made a shocking announcement: "Apple . . . needs help from other partners. Relationships that are destructive don't help anybody in this industry."[6] Microsoft, the company that had been Apple's main competitor for the last decade, was now going to be its partner.

Anderson had proposed the partnership with Microsoft. He wanted Jobs to convince Gates to develop a version of Microsoft Office for Macintosh. Office, a collection of productivity software that let users create documents, spreadsheets, and presentations, was one of the computer industry's most-used products. Earlier that year, Gates had refused to commit to this.

At Macworld, Gates loomed over Jobs on a giant screen as they announced the partnership between Apple and Microsoft.

But Anderson believed a deal with Microsoft was the key to Apple's survival.

So Jobs visited Gates and used his one piece of leverage to convince Gates to help Apple. Years earlier, Apple had sued Microsoft for patent violation, claiming Microsoft Windows copied the Macintosh graphical user interface. Although Gates contended that Xerox PARC had created this interface, he wanted the case settled. Jobs offered to drop the lawsuit if Microsoft committed to making Office for the Macintosh for five years and if it invested $150 million into Apple. Gates agreed.[7]

As Jobs laid out the details of the partnership with Microsoft in front of the Macworld audience, he ignored the frowns on some people's faces. Jobs introduced Bill Gates via a live video feed. Some people booed, but Gates did not notice as he laid out the details of Microsoft Office for the Mac. The audience quieted down. This was Apple's new future. By the end of the day, Apple's stock had jumped 33 percent.[8]

TEMPORARILY PERMANENT CEO

On September 16, 1997, Jobs announced he would take over as Apple's interim CEO. He refused to accept a salary or sign a contract, but he had full control of the company. This was supposed to be a temporary position while Jobs and the board hunted for a permanent CEO, but the board stopped seriously searching. People who knew Jobs during his first stint at Apple worried that the erratic, impulsive behavior that got him pushed out of Apple might return. However, Jobs had matured and now acted like a smart manager of a major corporation.

One of Jobs's priorities was to trim down the company's wide range of products. He called product teams into a conference room and demanded managers justify why their product was essential. This revealed that

Apple was making multiple versions of the same device. There were so many versions of the Macintosh that even Jobs could not keep them straight. Jobs cut 70 percent of Apple's products and 3,000 employees.[9]

THINK DIFFERENT

Jobs contacted Lee Clow, the advertising agency executive who had created the famous 1984 Super Bowl commercial for the Macintosh. Jobs told Clow he needed an ad campaign to remind consumers of what Apple originally stood for—creativity and individualism. Clow's ad agency brainstormed ideas for the campaign. The team came up with the slogan "Think Different," deciding to link Apple's brand to famous people known for being changemakers.

The Think Different campaign appeared on billboards and posters, on television, and in print. Each ad featured a black-and-white image of an iconic person such as Mohandas Gandhi or Cesar Chavez. The picture was accompanied by the slogan "Think Different" and the Apple logo. The Think Different campaign was a huge success. It ran for five years and won many awards, including an Emmy.

iMAC

As powerful as the Think
Different ads were, they would
not have mattered if Apple had
not turned out a great product.
Apple had to release something
new and revolutionary and
had to launch it soon. Neither
customers nor investors were
going to wait long for Apple
to prove it was worth a second
chance. The man who was key
to developing just what Apple
needed was Jony Ive, the head
of Apple's design team.

The first time Jobs walked
into Apple's design lab, Ive
was nervous. The designer was convinced Jobs was there
to fire him because the company's products were not
very good. But the two men established an immediate
connection. Jobs recognized Ive's talent and Ive realized
Jobs cared as much about Apple's products as its profits.
Together they went to work on developing Apple's next
hit computer, the iMac.

Jobs wanted a personal computer that would be simple and easy to use right out of the box. He also wanted it to have a distinctive design and to sell for no more than $1,200. To achieve this, Apple's engineers and designers worked hand in hand. Technologically, the iMac was not much different from Macintosh computers that had come before. But its look was fresh and new. The iMac's hardware was encased in translucent colored plastic. Users could see inside to the guts of the computer. Ive said the design team was "trying to convey a sense of the computer being changeable based on your needs, to be like a chameleon."[11]

A handle nestled into the top of the iMac was designed to make the machine approachable by creating a relationship between machine and user. The iMac did not intimidate like other computers because the user could pick it up like a suitcase. Ive designed a curved frame for the iMac, which he thought made the computer look like "it's just about to hop off [the desk] and go somewhere."[12]

Most computers at this time had a floppy disk drive, but the iMac had a CD-ROM drive. CDs could store vastly more data than the older floppy disk technology.

The introduction of the iMac stunned the computer industry and set the company on a path toward success.

The iMac had a 15-inch (38 cm) monitor and was equipped to easily connect to the internet. It also got rid of a variety of ports, replacing them with a new standard connection called Universal Serial Bus (USB). This type of port would soon become the common way to connect devices to computers. The iMac was among the first personal computers to include it as a standard feature.

Apple had proven it still "thought different." The iMac was spunky and looked friendly. People who had been afraid of computers now wanted one. In the first six weeks it was available, 278,000 iMacs were sold. Nearly one million were sold by the end of 1998.[13] The iMac was the fastest-selling computer in Apple's history.

JONY IVE

Jony Ive grew up near London, England, and learned craftsmanship from his father, a silversmith and professor of design. Ive's father made a deal with his son. If Ive designed the plans for a project, his dad would help build it. Together they made furniture, a go-cart, and a tree house. Ive studied design at the Newcastle Polytechnic Institute and worked for a design consultant in the summers using a Macintosh computer as his tool.

In 1992, Ive was hired in Apple's design department. Within four years, he was the head of the department. When Jobs returned to lead Apple in 1997, he and Ive formed a close bond. Jobs described the designer as "wickedly intelligent" and the closest thing he had to a "spiritual partner at Apple."[14]

Ive's goal was to design simple, beautiful, and functional products. But a simple design is not easy. According to Ive, a designer must "deeply understand the essence of a product in order to be able to get rid of the parts that are not essential."[15] The iMac was the first result of the Ive-Jobs collaboration.

In 2018, Ive continued to be the chief of design at Apple and the most important person at the company except for CEO Cook. Ive's imprint can be seen on everything from the iPhone to the Apple Watch to the layout of Apple Stores.

Ive has often taken a public-facing role in introducing Apple's latest product designs.

CHAPTER **SIX**

SIMPLICITY

Not everyone could handle the pressure of working with Jobs. For all of 1997, Jobs did the work of both CEO and head of operations because the former operations head quit after working under Jobs for three months. Jobs did not like any of the candidates who applied for the position. Then, in 1998, he found Tim Cook.

CUTTING WASTE

Cook had worked in the computer industry for 16 years, including a long stint at IBM. Jobs liked what he saw in the mild-mannered man from Alabama right away. Not only did Cook have the management experience Jobs sought, but "he and I saw things exactly the same way," Jobs said. "He had the same vision I did."[1] Jobs offered Cook the position. Apple was still struggling financially in 1998. But five minutes into the interview, Cook knew he would say yes. He later described it as

Cook, *left*, would eventually become Apple's CEO.

"a once-in-a-lifetime opportunity to work for a creative genius."[2]

Cook quickly got to work improving the company's efficiency. First, he slashed Apple's inventory. The longer computers sat on warehouse shelves, the more their value dropped. Cook believed Apple should manage inventory like a dairy farm: "If it gets past its freshness date, you have a problem."[3] Cook closed ten of Apple's 19 warehouses. When he was hired, there was one month of inventory in Apple's warehouses. After 18 months on the job, Cook had cut inventory down to two days' worth.

One hundred companies supplied Apple—too many, in Cook's opinion. He slashed this number to 24 and negotiated better deals with these suppliers. Cook also reduced the time it took to manufacture a computer from four months to two. This move saved money and gave customers the latest available technology on their new machines.

THE SHOPPING EXPERIENCE

One part of the customer experience Jobs could not control was how products were sold in stores. He believed salespeople cared about their bonuses more than they

Apple's stores are known for their simple, minimalist appearance that spotlights the company's products.

did about which computer was best suited for a customer. Apple computers had innovative features and a higher price tag, so they needed knowledgeable salespeople to pitch them. What Apple needed was its own stores.

Ron Johnson, a former executive for retailer Target, was hired to head this project. During Johnson's second interview, he and Jobs drove to a nearby mall and walked around. At the time, computers were sold only in big-box stores located miles away from the mall, where land was cheaper. They decided that Apple might not be able to convince people to drive several miles to a store, but it could persuade mall customers to walk a few feet to an Apple Store.

The board of directors did not like the idea of Apple Stores, fearful they would lose money. Because Jobs felt so strongly about the project, one director suggested he build a prototype version so everyone could get a feel for how such a store would operate. So Jobs and Johnson rented a warehouse in Cupertino and met there every Tuesday for months to brainstorm.

The prototype was finished in January 2001. When the board visited the store for the first time, the directors unanimously approved going forward with the project. On May 19, 2001, more than 500 people lined up before dawn to be the first to enter Apple's store in an upscale mall in McClean, Virginia. When the doors opened, customers entered an airy, clean space. The wood floors were light and polished. Apple products were displayed on wall-length tables and on white, curved platforms. The same day, a second Apple Store opened in a mall in Glendale, California, a wealthy suburb of Los Angeles.

That weekend, nearly 8,000 people shopped at the two stores, purchasing $599,000 of merchandise.[4]

MUSIC REVOLUTION

Jobs loved music, but he did not immediately realize when young people started getting their music a whole new way. By 2000, youth were ripping music from CDs onto their computers. They also downloaded songs from file-sharing services like Napster. Apple searched for a way to enter the rapidly changing music industry.

APPLE STORES

By the end of 2001, another 23 Apple Stores had opened, their locations strategically selected based on the income in the area.[5] Customers could experiment with hardware and software. They could bring in their computers for service. The stores offered free seminars and other community events. Through its stores, Apple was creating a culture. By 2018, Apple had opened more than 500 retail stores in more than 20 countries.[6]

The company purchased Soundjam, an app created by two former Apple engineers. Soundjam was a database program capable of cataloging huge collections of music. Songs could be easily ripped from CDs, compressed into small audio files, and stored on a computer. For nine months, the Soundjam team members worked in top secret within Apple. They transformed Soundjam into Apple's own music app, called iTunes.

APPLE STORES
AROUND THE WORLD

ARCTIC OCEAN

SWEDEN

CANADA

UNITED STATES

NORTH ATLANTIC OCEAN

NORTH PACIFIC OCEAN

MEXICO

SOUTH PACIFIC OCEAN

BRAZIL

SOUTH ATLANTIC OCEAN

1 5 6
3 7 9
8
2 10

CHINA

SOUTH KOREA
JAPAN
TAIWAN
MACAO
HONG KONG

UNITED ARAB EMIRATES

SINGAPORE

INDIAN OCEAN

AUSTRALIA

N
W E
S

1. UNITED KINGDOM
2. SPAIN
3. FRANCE
4. BELGIUM
5. NETHERLANDS
6. GERMANY
7. SWITZERLAND
8. ITALY
9. AUSTRIA
10. TURKEY

Apple Stores around the world provide a place for Apple to sell its products directly to customers, provide repairs and service, and highlight how people can use its products in their daily lives.

On January 9, 2001, Jobs described the digital music revolution in his keynote speech at Macworld in San Francisco. The problem, according to Jobs, was that the available products to help consumers rip music, catalog it, and listen to it were very complex. "We're late to this party," Jobs admitted. "And we're about to do a leapfrog."[7] That leapfrog was iTunes.

This media management program allowed users to do all these tasks in one integrated application. Jobs described it as "really clean, really simple and far more powerful" than anything else available on the market.[8] Downloading iTunes was free for Mac users. The first week after iTunes was made available online, 275,000 copies were downloaded. Still, there was one other piece of the music puzzle. Users could catalog their music libraries on iTunes. But they used other companies' devices to listen to songs on the go. Apple began thinking about creating its own portable music player.

iPOD

In February 2001, Apple engineer Jon Rubinstein went to Japan to visit Toshiba, one of Apple's suppliers. Engineers there showed him a new product they were developing, a computer hard drive that held five gigabytes of storage and was the size of a silver dollar. Rubinstein wanted it. The MP3 players on the market at the time were hard to use and could store only about a dozen songs. Toshiba's drive could hold 1,000.[9]

Rubinstein called Jobs and said he had Apple's solution to making a portable music player. All he needed was a check for $10 million. Jobs gave it to him and Rubinstein negotiated an exclusive right to every drive Toshiba could make.

Jobs wanted the portable music player on the shelves that Christmas season, so the team worked around the clock. Rubinstein brought in entrepreneur Tony Fadell to help design the device. The prototype had a drive that held 1,000 songs and a battery that lasted long enough to play all 1,000. The user interface was a scroll wheel that allowed users to easily navigate between song titles, genres, and artists. Team members knew they had a hit because they all wanted a device like this themselves. The copywriting team suggested Apple name the device a Pod. Jobs added the "i."

The invitation to the iPod's unveiling on October 23, 2001, read, "Hint: It's not a Mac." Normally during launches, Jobs whipped a black cloth off a device that sat on a table in the middle of the stage. This time, Jobs described all the technical abilities of Apple's newest

The original iPod was not an immediate success, but subsequent models became some of the most popular devices in the world.

device and then said, "I happen to have one right here in my pocket." He reached into his jeans pocket and pulled out an iPod.[11]

The first iPods were also expensive. At $399, an iPod cost hundreds more than a CD player or MP3 player. A joke running on some blogs said iPod was short for "idiots price our devices."[12] In their first three months in stores, only 150,000 iPods sold, lower than Apple had forecast. So Jobs cut the price by $100 and introduced an improved version that held more songs and had a better scroll wheel. Apple proved it could respond quickly to market demands. Over the next few years it released the iPod Mini, the iPod Nano, and the iPod Shuffle. By 2004, the iPod made up 23 percent of Apple's revenue.[13]

CANCER, ROUND ONE

In the midst of this intensely creative time, Jobs felt sick. He often suffered from kidney stones, so he went to the doctor in the summer of 2003 for an ultrasound to see if he had another one. The doctor saw a shadow on the image and urged him to come in for tests. When Jobs returned that October, tests revealed a slowly growing cancerous tumor on his pancreas.

Doctors advised Jobs to have the tumor surgically removed before it spread, but he refused. To the dismay of his wife and close friends, Jobs was determined to fight the tumor with natural remedies. However, nine months later another scan showed the cancer had spread, and Jobs agreed to surgery.

On July 31, 2004, doctors removed Jobs's pancreas and part of his stomach and intestine. The day after surgery, Jobs notified Apple employees by email. He said Cook

Jobs returned to work in September 2004 following his surgery, welcoming customers to the first Apple ministore the next month.

would serve as acting CEO in his absence and that he would be back on the job by September. Jobs also lied to his staff. He said surgery was a "cure" for his type of cancer. But actually, during surgery the doctors found three tumors on his liver. Jobs began chemotherapy and kept his ongoing battle with cancer secret.

CHAPTER SEVEN

THREE IN ONE

Even though the sales of iPods were going through the roof in 2005, Jobs was worried. He told Apple's board, "The device that can eat our lunch is the cell phone."[1] If someone figured out how to make a cell phone that played music, the iPod would become irrelevant. Apple had to invent that technology first.

RESEARCH AND DEVELOPMENT

Around 2003, Jobs assigned Fadell, the man who had led development of the iPod, the task of creating a music-playing phone. Fadell created several prototypes, but none worked smoothly. One model used the iPod's wheel to navigate, but this was too clumsy for dialing phone numbers. Another prototype was like a videophone, but it was too sophisticated for the cellular networks of the time.

Jobs's announcement of the iPhone set the stage for Apple's incredible success in the years to come.

While Fadell's team worked on a phone, Project Purple was also underway. Jobs had learned that Microsoft was developing a portable PC that users could write on with a stylus, and he wanted Apple to get there first. Project Purple's goal was to invent an ultralight, tablet-sized computer with a touch screen. The Project Purple team ran into problems. Their models were too heavy or too expensive, or the batteries died too quickly.

Meanwhile, Apple researchers Greg Christie and Bas Ording were experimenting with a technology that had been stagnant for years. Christie had been a software engineer on the Newton. Users could write on the Newton with a stylus, but the device had flopped because it was unreliable and expensive. Jobs had abandoned the project, but Christie never lost his fascination with the possibilities of a touch screen user interface. He partnered with Ording, who had worked on the iPod's scroll-wheel user interface.

Touch screen technology had come a long way since the Newton, and the men eventually built a prototype. The problem was that the surface they built was the size of a conference-room table. When they showed the screen to Ive, the designer was not impressed. However, what could be done on the touch screen was amazing. Using both hands, Christie moved folders around and clicked icons. Ording shrank and enlarged documents and scrolled down the screen's horizontal edge. Ive insisted Jobs see the prototype. If they could figure out how to shrink it, the prototype could be Project Purple's solution.

By this time, Jobs was no longer excited about building a tablet. He understood what consumers really wanted was a better cell phone. Still, at Ive's urging, he went to look at the touch screen. Jobs was not impressed. Ive was disappointed when Jobs just shrugged. However, the device stuck in Jobs's mind. Over the next few days, he picked the brains of the engineering and design staff. Was there a way to use the prototype device's touch screen on a cell phone? Fadell thought the interface had potential, but the engineers wondered how they could shrink a screen the size of a table to a device that could fit into a pocket. "Go figure [it] out," Jobs ordered.[2]

The mission of Project Purple changed. The tablet was abandoned, and Jobs ordered the team to make "a really cool, really small, really thin phone" with a touch screen.[3] After a long period of trial and error, they came up with a phone intimately responsive to its user. If one wanted to type, a mini keyboard popped onto the screen. If one wanted to dial a number, a number pad appeared. All buttons vanished when watching a video. The phone was thin, sleek, and easy to use. It would be unlike any device that had ever been seen before.

LAST-MINUTE CHANGE

Shortly before the iPhone project was complete, Jobs decided he was unhappy with the product. He went to see Ive and confessed, "I just don't love it." At that point the phone's glass screen sat inside an aluminum case. Jobs wanted the glass screen to go as far to the edge as possible and told the design team they had to redesign it. Instead of whining, the team got to work. Jobs recalled it as one of his "proudest moments at Apple."[4]

UNVEILING THE iPHONE

On January 9, 2007, music blared as thousands of people poured into the Moscone Center in San Francisco for the annual Macworld trade show. Jobs strode onstage in his customary jeans and black turtleneck. The audience knew something big was coming, but Jobs took his time. For 30 minutes, he discussed Apple's product line. Finally, he launched into the news that everyone was waiting for.

"Every once in a while," Jobs said, "a revolutionary product comes along that changes everything. Today, we're introducing three revolutionary products of this class."[5] He explained that the first product was an iPod with touch controls. The audience cheered. He continued, describing the second device as a mobile phone. More cheers. The third, Jobs announced, was a revolutionary internet-communications device. The audience clapped.

Jobs described the three products again as an icon for each one flashed large on the screen. Then the icons came together and rotated as one image. "Are you getting it?" Jobs asked. "These are not three separate devices—this is one device! And we are calling it iPhone."[6] The iPhone launched five months later. Within a few years, all new smartphones used a touch screen interface.

iPAD

Once the iPhone's success was apparent, Jobs returned to the tablet project. He wanted the screen to be the main focal point for the device. Attention was paid to

The iPad brought the touch screen technology popularized by the iPhone to a much larger device.

the tiniest detail. Ive made 20 screen models of different shapes and sizes, and he and Jobs spent an afternoon picking them up and putting them down until one felt right.

A frenzy of excitement preceded the tablet's launch on January 27, 2010. The *Wall Street Journal* wrote, "The last time there was this much excitement about a tablet, it had some commandments written on it."[7] Instead of a table in the center of the stage, for this launch there was a comfy leather chair and a coffee table. Jobs talked about the iPhone and the iMac and asked, "Is there room for a third category of device in the middle?"[8]

Apple's answer was yes, and this device was the iPad. Jobs sat down in the easy chair and rested the iPad on his lap. "It's so much more intimate than a laptop and it's so much more capable than a smartphone," he said.[9]

Despite the excitement prior to the iPad's launch, the reaction after Jobs's demonstration was lukewarm. Some critics called it an iPhone on steroids. Gates dismissed the device completely, believing that a combination of voice control, a stylus, and a keyboard were better tools for a tablet than a touch screen. However, once the iPad went on sale in April 2010, it became a hit product. In less than one month, Apple sold one million iPads. Less than a year later, more than 15 million had been sold.

CANCER, ROUND TWO

During the iPad's launch, Jobs sat down in a leather chair to show the casual, intimate way an iPad fit into a person's life. The chair was also onstage because Jobs did not have the stamina to stand for long. In early 2008, doctors realized Jobs's cancer was spreading, and he was losing weight rapidly. With his pancreas gone, he needed to eat more and more often, but the cancer and pain medication reduced his appetite.

By 2009, the cancer had spread to Jobs's liver, and he needed a transplant. He wrote an open letter to staff on January 14, 2009, finally admitting that his health problems were complicated and he needed to take a medical leave. On March 21, Jobs received a liver transplant. He returned to work a few weeks later but never regained his appetite or stamina. When he announced the iPad in January 2010, he was thin and frail.

Doctors discovered new tumors in 2011. Finally, Jobs faced the inevitable. He was dying. The time had come to safeguard Apple's future. On August 24, 2011, Jobs was secretly wheeled into Apple's executive conference room prior to the beginning of a board meeting. The directors knew why Jobs was there, but Cook carried on with business. Then Jobs said he had something personal to say and he read from a prepared letter.

"I have always said if there ever came a day when I could no longer meet my duties and expectations as Apple's CEO, I would be the first to let you know. Unfortunately, that day has come."[10] Jobs recommended that Cook replace him. On October 5, 2011, Jobs died. He was 56 years old.

Jobs had been an extraordinary figure, and some predicted Apple would flounder after his death. However, Cook was an experienced business manager. He ended up taking Apple to greater financial heights than ever before. In the first five years of Cook's tenure as CEO, he doubled both Apple's revenues and its profits.

In his last public appearances in the summer of 2011, Jobs was strikingly thinner than he had been before.

CHAPTER EIGHT

CONTROVERSY

O
n December 2, 2015, two people with guns burst into a holiday party for employees of the San Bernardino, California, county health department. In minutes, 14 people were killed and 22 wounded. The attackers, a married couple, were killed by law enforcement as they fled the scene. The following day, the Federal Bureau of Investigation (FBI) searched the couple's home and found a cache of weapons, pipe bombs, and ammunition. They also found an iPhone. When the FBI tried to unlock the phone, they were blocked because they did not have the user's four-digit security code.

The FBI asked Apple for the security code, but Apple does not have users' personal codes. So the bureau asked Apple to create a technical backdoor to unlock the phone. Apple refused. This decision pitted the technology company against the federal government. The ensuing

Questions about privacy, security, and Apple's policy were highlighted following a December 2015 terrorist attack.

debate over how to balance privacy and security was one of several controversies Apple had to face in the second decade of the 2000s.

SECURITY VERSUS PRIVACY

After Cook denied the FBI's request to unlock the iPhone, the agency went to court. A judge issued a court order requiring Apple to create software that would let the FBI unlock the phone. The agency could have applied for this court order under a seal of silence, but it chose not to. The FBI wanted Americans to know that Apple was refusing to help prosecute domestic terrorism.

That was not how Apple viewed the situation. The company insisted it was not trying to defend the privacy of a dead terrorist. Instead, it was trying to defend the privacy of all iPhone users. Security experts agree that once such backdoor software is created, the security of every iPhone anywhere would be potentially compromised. The code could be accidentally released, or hackers could steal it. Authoritarian governments could use it to pry into citizens' personal data.

Apple did not stand alone in its fight to protect privacy. Major technology firms including Microsoft,

Amazon, and Google filed legal documents in support of the company's position. The United Nations High Commissioner for Human Rights and the former head of the National Security Agency also took Apple's side.

The FBI argued that Apple could have created a code tailored to just the terrorist's phone. But Apple insisted that once that code was created, knowledgeable computer programmers could modify it to attack other phones. Plus, Apple believed complying with the government's request would set a precedent. Law enforcement officials would return every time they needed access to a locked digital device for other cases, some not as dire as terrorism. Critics argued that Apple's security system was protecting terrorists as well as law-abiding citizens, and Cook agreed. He said, "We get that. But you don't take away the good for that sliver of bad. We've never been about that as a country."[1]

A DIFFERENT WORLD

When Apple refused to unlock the cell phone of the San Bernardino terrorists in 2016, President Barack Obama accused Apple of putting the nation's "phones above every other value."[2] Donald Trump, at the time a candidate for president, called for a boycott of Apple. James Comey, the director of the FBI in 2016, testified at a congressional hearing about the case. He said law enforcement protects the nation and that protection was enabled through court-ordered search warrants, like the one the FBI wanted Apple to follow. Comey admitted if the FBI did not get access to the terrorist's phone, "The world will not end, but it will be a different world."[3]

The battle between Apple and the FBI ended in March 2016 when the FBI dropped its charges against Apple. An anonymous outside group helped the agency hack into the terrorist's phone, and the FBI extracted the files it wanted. By the summer of 2018, the method used to get around the iPhone's barriers had not been disclosed.

WORKING CONDITIONS

One night in May 2011, chemical dust in a Foxconn factory in Chengdu, China, exploded. Two people were killed and a dozen injured. Foxconn manufactures a variety of Apple's products; this particular factory built iPads.

This was not the first explosion in a Chinese factory making a product that bore the Apple logo. Most tech companies manufacture their products in China. Apple contracts with suppliers such as Foxconn and Pegatron who hire local workers to make the devices sold in Apple Stores around the world.

Since 2005, Apple has had a code of conduct for its suppliers. This code requires that workers in factories that contract with Apple are treated with dignity and respect. The factories must guarantee health and safety standards and must be environmentally responsible. While this code looks good on paper, ensuring that suppliers comply with the code has been a challenge for Apple.

In 2012, the *New York Times* did an undercover investigation of conditions in Apple factories in China. It discovered working conditions that would be illegal in the United States. Employees at Apple's suppliers worked seven days a week, 12 hours a day. They were compelled to use toxic chemicals, and hazardous waste was illegally dumped.

Cook has addressed the issue of Apple's labor problems more boldly than his predecessor did, perhaps because of Cook's own life experience. As a youth, he

Reports of unsafe working conditions in the Chinese factories that produced Apple's products drew more scrutiny to the company and its suppliers.

worked at a paper mill and an aluminum plant and knows firsthand how hard factory labor is. Shortly after taking over as Apple's CEO, Cook toured a Foxconn factory where workers had been committing suicide because of work-related stress. In 2012, Apple released the names of 156 of its suppliers, something the company had refused to do before. With supply companies' names in the public record, labor associations can investigate them more easily. That year Apple also became the first tech company to join the Fair Labor Association, a nonprofit group that monitors labor conditions around the world.

Despite these reforms, Apple still gets accused of not doing enough to improve working conditions. In 2014, the British Broadcasting Company (BBC) aired a report of an undercover investigation of Apple's Pegatron supplier in Shanghai, China. The exposé revealed video of workers falling asleep on the job and reports of people working 18 days in a row. Footage of Indian children mining by hand in India revealed that Apple has failed to monitor companies that provide materials to its suppliers.

Apple responded quickly and strongly to the BBC report. Jeff Williams, Apple's vice president of operations, said the company was "deeply offended" by the BBC's report. Williams insisted it was common practice for employees at these Chinese factories to nap during their breaks and insisted the company will continue to work with its suppliers to identify problems like underage workers in mines. He insisted Apple has made continuous improvements to working conditions in Asia, but he acknowledged "our work is never done."[4]

TAXES

In the American tax system, the more income a company makes, the more money it pays in taxes. At least that is how the system is supposed to work. From 2008 to 2018, Apple has been steadily increasing in value, and in early 2018 it was worth almost $1 trillion. However, during that decade, Apple paid relatively little in taxes.

When a Senate committee discovered this fact in 2013,

TAX DODGING

In 2016, the European Union (EU) accused Apple of tax dodging. A study by the EU concluded that the business practices of major global corporations cost EU countries between $54.5 billion and $76.4 billion a year in lost tax revenue. A 2016 study by the Center for Tax Justice found that Apple had $181.1 billion in offshore profits held by subsidiaries in Ireland but paid a tax rate of only 2.3 percent.[5] In the fall of 2017, the EU sued the government of Ireland because it had not recovered this money from Apple. Under a worst-case scenario, Apple could wind up having to pay billions in back taxes and penalties to resolve this dispute.

Cook testified in 2013 that Apple pays all the taxes that it is legally obligated to pay.

senators accused Apple of using "gimmicks" that included using offshore subsidiaries to lower its tax rate to only 0.05 percent. The chairman of the Senate panel, Carl Levin from Michigan, called these subsidiaries "ghost companies." Subsidiaries often have no employees and no real offices. They exist to shelter money in countries that have very low corporate tax rates, such as Ireland.

One of Apple's Irish subsidiaries made $30 billion in profit between 2009 and 2012 but paid zero taxes.[6]

Cook appeared before the Senate panel on May 20, 2013, and he told Senator Levin that he wanted the American people to hear Apple's explanation from him. Apple, Cook said, has paid "all the taxes we owe—every single dollar."[7] Then he turned the tables. Apple's methods of reducing its tax burden were completely legal because the old-fashioned American tax code had not kept pace with the digital age. Congress is the body with the power to change the law.

Cook maintained that American corporations that do business globally are penalized by the high corporate tax rate for money kept in the United States, so they shelter it in offshore accounts. He admitted it was true that Apple pays very little taxes on products it sells outside the United States, but it pays a 30.5 percent tax rate on goods it sells inside the United States.[8]

Apple's tax bill is destined to change. Congress passed a tax-overhaul law that went into effect on January 1, 2018, reducing the corporate tax rate. Cook welcomed that change. One of his future goals is to invest heavily in the United States.

CHAPTER NINE

MISSION FOR THE FUTURE

I n a 2017 interview with *Fortune* magazine, Cook was asked how Apple changes the world. He answered with two words: "Our products."[1] For more than 40 years, Apple has made its reputation by creating tools for people to do things they otherwise could not do. New products are on Apple's horizon, but the company is also expanding its mission, recasting its image, and transforming its place in the world.

IN THE PIPELINE

Technology known as artificial intelligence (AI) is used to create computer systems that can do things that are usually considered tasks for humans. These include recognizing images, translating languages, and making decisions. AI will be a major part of Apple's future.

Apple's artificial intelligence assistant, Siri, is a key part of the company's smart speaker product, called HomePod.

Apple was among the early smartphone manufacturers to use AI. In 2011, Apple released the iPhone 3GS. This was its first phone to include Siri, a virtual assistant. Siri listened to voice commands, searched the web for information, and verbally answered the user. But users criticized Siri's shortcomings. Its abilities were limited, and they did not seem to improve with time. Meanwhile, Apple's competitors rapidly improved their own AI offerings.

In 2014, Amazon launched a smart speaker featuring a virtual assistant named Alexa. Google followed with its own product, featuring Google Assistant, in 2016. These devices play music, radio, and podcasts, but they also include microphones that listen for the user's voice. The user can choose songs, ask questions, and control home appliances with the spoken word. Amazon soon commanded the greatest share of this market with its line of Echo devices, but Google, with its Home line of speakers, was close behind. Apple did not release its own smart speaker, the HomePod, until 2018.

While Apple is lagging in the smart speaker market, the company is performing better in health technology. Its smart watch, the Apple Watch, can detect a user's heart rate. It can recognize irregular heart activity, letting the user know if he or she should see a doctor. In January 2018, Apple released the Health App for the iPhone. The company collaborated with the health-care community to allow users to download their medical records from different institutions and store this data on their iPhones. A user can see immunizations, allergies, medications, procedures, and lab results on one screen. The user gets to decide who else can see the information.

ECONOMIC IMPACT

After years of criticism for holding its money offshore, Apple intends to make a major investment in the United States. A few weeks after President Donald Trump signed a major tax-reform bill into law in December 2017, Apple announced that over the next five years, it would contribute $350 billion to the American economy.

SCREEN ADDICTION

In early 2018, two major shareholders urged Apple to study the reportedly dangerous effects of American youth spending so much time on their smartphones. In response, Apple said it had "new features and enhancements planned for the future, to . . . make these [parental control] tools even more robust."[2] Cook also addressed the issue and put the blame on social media. He believes parents should limit their children's phone usage. "I'm not a person that says we've achieved success if you're using [our devices] all the time," Cook said. "I don't subscribe to that at all."[3]

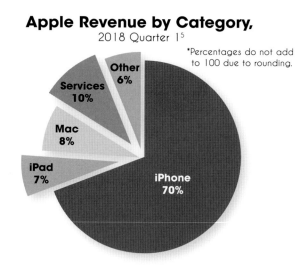

Apple Revenue by Category,
2018 Quarter 1[5]

*Percentages do not add to 100 due to rounding.

- Other 6%
- Services 10%
- Mac 8%
- iPad 7%
- iPhone 70%

Apple introduced the iPhone in 2007. By 2018, the device represented the vast majority of the company's revenue. Desktop computers, the devices that gave the company its start in the 1970s, made up less than 10 percent of income.

The new tax law grants corporations a one-time deal to return cash held abroad at a lower tax rate than normal. Apple will bring home most of the money it holds abroad and make a single tax payment of $38 billion. Cook announced some of this money would be used to create 20,000 new jobs in America. "We have a deep sense of responsibility," Cook said, "to give back to our country."[4]

TAKE A STAND

During a business forum in September 2017, Cook said that all people have values and a company was nothing more than a collection of people. "So by extension," he explained, "all companies should have values."[6] In recent years, Apple has shown it is a company committed to improving the environment, education, and civil rights.

Apple went from lagging behind other corporations on environmental issues to becoming a leader in green energy. In 2011, the environmental watchdog group Greenpeace ranked Apple last out of 16 companies in its *Guide to Greener Electronics*. The main reason for this poor ranking was because Apple relied on coal to power its servers, and it used a lot of electricity.

The company now runs all its data centers and stores on renewable energy. In 2015, Apple launched a plan to help its Asian suppliers switch to clean energy, too. It sought to do this by coordinating deals with Chinese firms to sell wind power to factories in their provinces.

In 2017, Apple pledged to work toward the day when all its products would be made from recycled or renewable materials. However, the company does not yet know how it will accomplish such a difficult task. "We're actually doing something we rarely do . . . announce a goal before we've completely figured out how to do it," an Apple spokesperson said.[7]

In 2014, some shareholders criticized the cost of these environmental changes, claiming they would not show a good return on investment. This angered Cook. "If you want me to do things only for ROI [return on investment] reasons," he stated, "you should get out of this stock."[8] Greenpeace likes the direction in which Apple is headed. In 2017, the group gave Apple an A rating.

Apple is also investing in American education. In 2015, the company joined President Obama's "ConnectED Initiative," which provides technology to poor schools. Apple donated $100 million in iPads and taught teachers how to use them.

Apple also created a computer-coding curriculum for grades K–12 that is being taught in after-school clubs in urban districts. "We believe education is a great equalizer," Cook said in a 2017 interview. "We think that coding is sort of the second language for everyone in the world."[9] This knowledge will open up experiences for students and also create a pool of young innovators who might one day help Apple discover its next great thing.

Under Cook's leadership, Apple has taken a public stance on controversial issues, including immigration. In early 2017, President Trump issued a temporary ban on immigration from several countries. The administration stated that the ban was due to a risk of terrorism from those nations, but critics contended that the ban would be discriminatory, in particular against Muslims. Apple joined more than 100 other tech companies in supporting a legal challenge to this ban.

SPACESHIP

Months before his death, on June 17, 2011, Jobs appeared before the Cupertino City Council to propose building a new Apple headquarters on the city's northern border. "I think we have a shot," Jobs said, "of building the best office building in the world."[10]

Construction on Apple Park, sometimes known as the Spaceship Campus for its flying saucer shape, was completed in the fall of 2017. A 1,000-seat auditorium named for Jobs sits on one of the highest points in the park. The main headquarters building is a huge circular structure of

DOING FOR OTHERS

An intensely private man, Cook came out publicly as gay in a 2014 essay he wrote for *Bloomberg* magazine. Cook said the words of Dr. Martin Luther King Jr. inspired him. King once asked his followers to think about what they were doing for others. When Cook asked himself this question, he realized his desire for privacy had kept him from using his platform to help others who faced discrimination because of their sexual orientation. "So let me be clear," Cook wrote, "I'm proud to be gay, and I consider being gay among the greatest gifts God has given me."[11]

curved glass. It is called the Ring. White canopies shaped like fins protrude from the glass on each of the four floors, giving the structure a science-fictional feel. The inner border of the Ring is a walkway where people stroll the three-quarter-mile (1.2 km) perimeter. Rather than one main lobby, there are nine entrances into the Ring. One of these opens into a café with a huge atrium that encompasses open ceilings that stretch the entire four floors of the structure. Two massive glass doors open from the café onto a patio.

Form follows function with the new headquarters just as it does with Apple's products. The inner layout of the building is open, with most employees working inside glass-walled pods. There are pods for individual work, pods for team projects, and pods for socializing. This design is supposed to foster collaboration.

Apple Park contains a visitor center, Apple Store, and public café. On-site is a fitness center, a research-and-development facility, walking trails, an underground parking garage, and an orchard, meadow, and pond. One thousand bicycles are kept on-site for staff to use on campus, and electric golf carts and shuttles are also available. The facility is powered completely

The enormous Apple Park facility had an estimated budget of $5 billion.

by sustainable energy, mostly from 805,000 square feet (74,800 sq m) of solar panels that line the tops of the buildings. For Ive, the new headquarters reflects what Apple is as a company. "This is our home," he said, "and everything we make in the future is going to start here."[12]

Apple began in a garage in 1976. Four decades later, it was one of the world's largest companies. Throughout its history, it has gone through turbulent times and triumphant moments. The central vision of Jobs and Wozniak—creating a truly personal computer—proved to be one of the defining advances of the modern era. By melding sophisticated technology with innovative design, Apple has become one of today's tech titans.

TIMELINE

1971
Steve Jobs and Stephen Wozniak meet.

1975
Wozniak attends his first meeting of the Homebrew Club on March 5, reigniting his passion for computers; Wozniak completes a prototype of the Apple I on June 29.

1976
Apple Computer Company is registered in California as a business on April 1.

1977
The Apple II is introduced to the world at a computer fair in San Francisco on April 16.

1984
The Macintosh computer is launched on January 24.

1985
Jobs resigns from Apple on September 17.

1993
Under pressure from Apple's board, John Sculley resigns as CEO.

1996
In December, Apple purchases Jobs's company NeXT and Jobs returns as an informal adviser to Apple's chairman of the board.

1997

Jobs announces a partnership with Microsoft at Macworld in August; on September 16, Jobs is named interim CEO of Apple, a position that becomes permanent.

1998

The iMac is launched.

2001

The first Apple Stores open on May 19; the iPod is launched on October 23.

2007

The first iPhone is announced on January 9.

2010

The iPad is released.

2011

Tim Cook is named CEO of Apple on August 24 after Jobs steps down due to illness; Jobs dies on October 5.

2017

Apple releases the iPhone X, the first iPhone to use facial-recognition software.

ESSENTIAL **FACTS**

KEY PLAYERS
FOUNDERS
- Stephen Wozniak, Steve Jobs

CEOs
- Michael Scott (1977–1981)
- Mike Markkula (1981–1983)
- John Sculley (1983–1993)
- Michael Spindler (1993–1996)
- Gil Amelio (1996–1997)
- Steve Jobs (1997–2011)
- Tim Cook (from 2011)

KEY STATISTICS
- In 1977, Apple was worth $5,309. By the end of 1980 it was valued at $1.79 billion. In 2018, it was valued at $911.906 billion.
- In 1996, Apple purchased Steve Jobs's company NeXT for $400 million in order to get its operating system.
- In the first month after the iPad went on sale in April 2010, Apple sold one million iPads; less than one year later, 15 million had been sold.
- In January 2018, Apple announced it would invest $350 billion into the United States economy over five years.

IMPACT ON HISTORY

Apple helped bring about the personal computer revolution with devices such as the Apple II and the Macintosh. Later, it helped upend the music industry, pushing it into the digital era with iTunes and the iPod. In 2007, it changed the smartphone landscape forever with the iPhone. Throughout its history, Apple has sought to mix the latest technology with a sophisticated design sensibility.

QUOTE

"The people who are crazy enough to think they can change the world, are the ones who do."

—Apple's Think Different advertising campaign

GLOSSARY

CEO
Chief executive officer of a company; the person in a company with the most authority.

circuit board
A thin, rigid board on which electronic circuits are printed or installed.

data center
A building designed to house large numbers of computers, with special attention paid to cooling systems, consistent electricity service, and network connectivity.

division
An operating unit of a business.

graphical user interface
A visual way of interacting with a computer using menus, icons, and windows.

hack
To secretly get access to the files on a computer or network in order to get information or cause damage.

hardware
The physical parts of the computer, including the keyboard and monitor, and also parts inside the computer, such as the hard drive and memory.

operating system
The basic software on a computer that allows other software programs to work with the computer's hardware.

port
A socket on a computer into which a device or cable can be plugged.

profit
The revenue a company gets to keep in earnings after costs are paid.

schematic
A diagram of an electronic circuit.

server
A computer in a network that is used to provide services to other computers in the network.

ADDITIONAL **RESOURCES**

SELECTED BIBLIOGRAPHY

Isaacson, Walter. *Steve Jobs*. Simon, 2011.

Schlender, Brent and Rick Tetzeli. *Becoming Steve Jobs: The Evolution of a Reckless Upstart into a Visionary Leader.* Crown, 2015.

Wozniak, Steve, with Gina Smith. *iWoz: Computer Geek to Cult Icon.* Norton, 2006.

FURTHER READINGS

Lusted, Marcia Amidon. *Apple: The Company and Its Visionary Founder, Steve Jobs.* Abdo, 2012.

Naber, Therese. *How the Computer Changed History*. Abdo, 2016.

ONLINE RESOURCES

Booklinks
NONFICTION NETWORK
FREE! ONLINE NONFICTION RESOURCES

To learn more about Apple, visit **abdobooklinks.com**. These links are routinely monitored and updated to provide the most current information available.

MORE INFORMATION

For more information on this subject, contact or visit the following organizations:

APPLE PARK VISITOR CENTER
10600 N. Tantau Avenue
Cupertino, CA 95014
408-961-1560
The visitors' center of Apple's headquarters includes a café, store, and exhibitions.

COMPUTER HISTORY MUSEUM
1401 N. Shoreline Boulevard
Mountain View, CA 94043
650-810-1010
computerhistory.org
The Computer History Museum is dedicated to preserving computer history and is home to the largest international collection of computing artifacts in the world.

SOURCE **NOTES**

CHAPTER 1. FIRST IN LINE

1. Robert Channick. "iPhone X Crowds Prove It's a Must-Have for Apple Fans, Even at $999." *Chicago Tribune*, 3 Nov. 2017, chicagotribune.com. Accessed 11 Mar. 2018.

2. Rebecca McClay. "What Makes Apple So Valuable?" *Investopedia*, 19 Jan. 2018, investopedia.com. Accessed 11 Mar. 2018.

3. Josh Lipton and Anita Balakrishnan. "Apple Apologizes for iPhone Slowdowns and Offers $29 Battery Replacements." *CNBC*, 28 Dec. 2017, cnbc.com. Accessed 11 Mar. 2018.

CHAPTER 2. APPLE'S ROOTS

1. Kathleen Elkins. "The First Project Steve Jobs and Steve Wozniak Worked On Was a High School Prank." *Chicago Tribune*, 28 Feb. 2017, cnbc.com. Accessed 24 Feb. 2018.

2. Jim Aley. "Jobs, Who Built Most Valuable Technology Company, Dies at 56." *Bloomberg*, 6 Oct. 2011, bloomberg.com. Web. Accessed 6 Mar. 2018.

3. Steve Wozniak with Gina Smith. *iWoz: Computer Geek to Cult Icon*. Norton, 2006. 156.

4. Wozniak with Smith, *iWoz*, 172.

5. Wozniak with Smith, *iWoz*, 174.

6. Wozniak with Smith, *iWoz*, 177.

7. Wozniak with Smith, *iWoz*, 185.

8. Harry McCracken. "Apple II Forever: A 35th-Anniversary Tribute to Apple's First Iconic Product." *Time*, 16 Apr. 2012, techland.time.com. Accessed 26 Feb. 2018.

9. Walter Isaacson. *Steve Jobs*. Simon, 2011. 81.

10. Brent Schlender and Rick Tetzeli. *Becoming Steve Jobs: The Evolution of a Reckless Upstart into a Visionary Leader*. Crown, 2015. 60.

11. Isaacson, *Steve Jobs*, 103–104.

12. Wozniak with Smith, *iWoz*, 42.

CHAPTER 3. FAILURE AND SUCCESS

1. Malcolm Gladwell. "Creation Myth." *New Yorker*, 16 May 2011, newyorker.com. Accessed 10 July 2018.

2. Brent Schlender and Rick Tetzeli. *Becoming Steve Jobs: The Evolution of a Reckless Upstart into a Visionary Leader*. Crown, 2015. 72.

3. Schlender and Tetzeli, *Becoming Steve Jobs*, 73.

4. "Apple III Chaos: Apple's First Failure." *LowEnd Mac*, 28 Apr. 2004, lowendmac.com. Accessed 17 Mar. 2018.

5. Anna Mazarakis and Alyson Shontell. "Former Apple CEO John Sculley Is Working on a Startup That He Thinks Could Become Bigger Than Apple." *Business Insider*, 10 Aug. 2017, businessinsider.com. Accessed 17 Mar. 2018.

6. Steven Levy. "The Birth of the Mac: *Rolling Stone*'s 1984 Feature on Steve Jobs and His Whiz Kids." *Rolling Stone*, 1 Mar. 1984, rollingstone.com. Accessed 16 Feb. 2018.

7. Levy, "The Birth of the Mac."

8. Matt Kapko. "History of Apple and Microsoft: 4 Decades of Peaks and Valleys." *CIO*, 7 Oct. 2015, cio.com. Accessed 22 Feb. 2018.

9. "Apple 1984 Super Bowl Commercial Introducing Macintosh Computer." *YouTube*, 25 Jan. 2010, youtube.com. Accessed 18 Feb. 2018.

10. Chris Higgins. "Apple's Iconic '1984' Superbowl Commercial Was Almost Canceled." *Business Insider*, 31 Jan. 2012, businessinsider.com. Accessed 5 Mar. 2018.

11. "Steve Jobs Introduces the Original Macintosh—Apple Shareholder Event (1984)." *YouTube*, 21 Dec. 2013, youtube.com. Accessed 18 Mar. 2018.

12. Levy, "The Birth of the Mac."

13. Walter Isaacson. *Steve Jobs*. Simon, 2011. 181.

14. Schlender and Tetzeli, *Becoming Steve Jobs*, 86.

15. Isaacson, *Steve Jobs*, 197.

CHAPTER 4. A BRUISED APPLE

1. Walter Isaacson. *Steve Jobs*. Simon, 2011. 200.

2. Isaacson, *Steve Jobs*, 216.

3. Isaacson, *Steve Jobs*, 295.

4. Matt Kapko. "History of Apple and Microsoft: 4 Decades of Peaks and Valleys." *CIO*, 7 Oct. 2015, cio.com. Accessed 22 Feb. 2018.

5. Kapko, "History of Apple and Microsoft."

6. John Markoff. "Marketer's Dream, Engineer's Nightmare." *New York Times*, 12 Dec. 1993, nytimes.com. Accessed 27 Feb. 2018.

7. Brent Schlender and Wilton Woods. "Something's Rotten in Cupertino." *Fortune*, 3 Mar. 1997, fortune.com. Accessed 19 Mar. 2018.

8. Schlender and Woods, "Something's Rotten in Cupertino."

CHAPTER 5. REGENERATION

1. Walter Isaacson. *Steve Jobs*. Simon, 2011. 306.

2. Isaacson, *Steve Jobs*, 309.

3. Isaacson, *Steve Jobs*, 317.

4. Isaacson, *Steve Jobs*, 319–321.

5. Isaacson, *Steve Jobs*, 322.

6. Isaacson, *Steve Jobs*, 323.

7. Brent Schlender and Rick Tetzeli. *Becoming Steve Jobs: The Evolution of a Reckless Upstart into a Visionary Leader*. Crown, 2015. 210–211.

8. Isaacson, *Steve Jobs*, 326.

9. Isaacson, *Steve Jobs*, 339.

10. Schlender and Tetzeli, *Becoming Steve Jobs*, 220.

11. Isaacson, *Steve Jobs*, 350.

12. Isaacson, *Steve Jobs*, 349.

13. Isaacson, *Steve Jobs*, 356.

14. Isaacson, *Steve Jobs*, 342.

15. Isaacson, *Steve Jobs*, 343.

CHAPTER 6. SIMPLICITY

1. Walter Isaacson. *Steve Jobs*. Simon, 2011. 360.

2. Isaacson, *Steve Jobs*, 360.

3. Adam Lashinsky. "Tim Cook: The Genius behind Steve." *Fortune*, 24 Nov. 2008, fortune.com. Accessed 19 Mar. 2018.

4. Benj Edwards. "A Tale of Two Apple Stores (The First Two)." *Macworld*, 19 May 2011, macworld.com. Accessed 19 Mar. 2018.

5. Edwards, "A Tale of Two Apple Stores."

6. "Apple Stores." *MacRumors*, n.d., macrumors.com. Accessed 20 Mar. 2018.

7. "Steve Jobs Introduces iTunes & PowerBook G4 Titanium—Macworld SF (2001)." *YouTube*, 23 Dec. 2013, youtube.com. Accessed 20 Mar. 2018.

8. "Steve Jobs Introduces iTunes & PowerBook G4 Titanium."

9. Isaacson, *Steve Jobs*, 384–385.

10. Isaacson, *Steve Jobs*, 395–402.

11. Isaacson, *Steve Jobs*, 390–392.

12. Isaacson, *Steve Jobs*, 390–393.

13. Arik Hesseldahl. "The iPod in Perspective." *Forbes*, 15 Oct. 2004, forbes.com. Accessed 20 Mar. 2018.

CHAPTER 7. THREE IN ONE

1. Walter Isaacson. *Steve Jobs*. Simon, 2011. 465.

2. Brent Schlender and Rick Tetzeli. *Becoming Steve Jobs: The Evolution of a Reckless Upstart into a Visionary Leader*. Crown, 2015. 311.

3. Schlender and Tetzeli, *Becoming Steve Jobs*, 311.

4. Isaacson, *Steve Jobs*, 472.

5. "Steve Jobs Introducing the iPhone at MacWorld 2007." *YouTube*, 2 Dec. 2010, youtube.com. Accessed 21 Mar. 2018.

6. "Steve Jobs Introducing the iPhone at MacWorld 2007."

7. Isaacson. *Steve Jobs*, 393.

8. "Steve Jobs Introduces Original iPad—Apple Special Event (2010)." *YouTube*, 30 Dec. 2013, youtube.com. Accessed 21 Mar. 2018.

9. "Steve Jobs Introduces Original iPad."

10. Schlender and Tetzeli, *Becoming Steve Jobs*, 558.

CHAPTER 8. CONTROVERSY

1. Lev Grossman. "Inside Apple CEO Tim Cook's Fight with the FBI." *Time*, 17 Mar. 2016, time.com. Accessed 21 Mar. 2018.

2. Grossman, "Inside Apple CEO Tim Cook's Fight with the FBI."

3. Grossman, "Inside Apple CEO Tim Cook's Fight with the FBI."

4. Matt Clinch. "Apple's Tim Cook Slams BBC Report." *CNBC*, 19 Dec. 2014, cnbc.com. Accessed 22 Mar. 2018.

5. Josie Cox. "EU Takes Ireland to Court Over $15bn Apple Back Taxes." *Independent*, 4 Oct. 2017, independent.co.uk. Accessed 22 Mar. 2018.

6. Tony Romm. "Senate Probers: Apple Sheltered $44B." *Politico*, 20 May 2013, politico.com. Accessed 22 Mar. 2018.

7. Nelson D. Schwartz and Brian X. Chen. "Disarming Senators, Apple Chief Eases Tax Tensions." *New York Times*, 21 Mar 2013, nytimes.com. Accessed 22 Mar. 2018.

8. Schwartz and Chen, "Disarming Senators, Apple Chief Eases Tax Tensions."

CHAPTER 9. MISSION FOR THE FUTURE

1. Adam Lashinsky. "Tim Cook on How Apple Champions the Environment, Education, and Health Care." *Fortune*, 11 Sept. 2017, fortune.com. Accessed 23 July 2018.

2. Jeremy Horowitz. "Apple Will Address Kids' iPhone Addiction with Enhanced iOS Parental Controls." *Venture Beat*, 9 Jan. 2018, venturebeat.com. Accessed 21 Mar. 2018.

3. Jeremy Horowitz. "Apple CEO Tim Cook Blames Social Media and Technology 'Overuse' after iPhone Addiction Criticisms." *Venture Beat*, 19 Jan. 2018, venturebeat.com. Accessed 21 Mar. 2018.

4. Jason Snell. "Apple Q1 2018 Earnings: Record Revenue, Beating the Estimates." *Six Colors*, 1 Feb. 2018, sixcolors.com. Accessed 10 July 2018.

5. Daisuke Wakabayashi and Brian X. Chen. "Apple, Capitalizing on New Tax Law, Plans to Bring Billions in Cash Back to U.S." *New York Times*, 17 Jan. 2018, nytimes.com. Accessed 22 Mar. 2018.

6. "Tim Cook: Corporations Should Have Values." *CNN Tech*, 20 Sept. 2017, money.cnn.com. Accessed 23 Mar. 2018.

7. Arjun Karpal. "Apple Pledges to Make Products Like the iPhone from Only Recycled Material and End Mining." *CNBC*, 20 Apr. 2017, cnbc.com. Accessed 26 Mar. 2018.

8. David Price. "Why Apple Was Bad for the Environment (and Why That's Changing)." *MacWorld*, 3 Jan. 2017, macworld.co.uk. Accessed 26 Mar. 2018.

9. Lashinsky, "Tim Cook on How Apple Champions the Environment, Education, and Health Care."

10. Stephen Levy. "One More Thing: Inside Apple's Insanely Great (or Just Insane) New Mothership." *Wired*, 16 May 2017, wired.com. Accessed 26 Mar. 2018.

11. Tim Cook. "Tim Cook Speaks Out." *Bloomberg*, 30 Oct. 2014, bloomberg.com. Accessed 22 Mar. 2018.

12. Levy, "One More Thing."

INDEX

ABOUT THE **AUTHOR**

JUDY DODGE CUMMINGS

Judy Dodge Cummings is the author of more than 20 books for young readers. She lives and writes in southern Wisconsin.

ABOUT THE **CONSULTANT**

ANTHONY ROTOLO

Anthony Rotolo was a college professor for more than ten years, teaching at Syracuse University. He taught courses in technology and media, including the very first college class on social media. He is now studying for a PhD in psychology and researching how social media affects people and society.